T0137698

A Must Read for all businesses and organizations
who want to survive in this economy

CORPORATE
TIME THEFT

You Can't Afford to Ignore It

GRACE CHANDY

AND

ZEN THARANI

Practical approach to saving your organization money

Order this book online at www.trafford.com
or email orders@trafford.com
Most Trafford titles are also available at major online book retailers.

Printed in the United States of America.

ISBN: 978-1-4269-3300-4 (sc)
ISBN: 978-1-4269-3301-1 (hc)
ISBN: 978-1-4669-1593-0 (e)

Library of Congress Control Number: 2012905222

Trafford rev. 03/28/2012

   www.trafford.com

North America & international
toll-free: 1 888 232 4444 (USA & Canada)
phone: 250 383 6864 ♦ fax: 812 355 4082

Dedicated to your prosperity

PREFACE

We remember clearly how we felt when we first realized the effects of Time Theft on organizations. As we reminisce, a recognizable scene from a popular Hollywood movie comes to mind: the main character is offered a choice between two pills. One pill will open up his eyes to a world that he never knew existed. The second pill will provide the comfort of complacency and return him back to his normal day-to-day life with no recollection of this opportunity to know more. We can't tell you how happy we are that we chose the pill that would open our eyes to the concept of Time Theft and its impact on organizations.

The purpose of this book is simple: we will quantify the prevalence of Time Theft, show you how to identify it, and give you some strategies to contain it.

This book is intended to be a reality check and to get you thinking and talking about the effects of *Corporate Time Theft* in your organization. We have written this book using the same principle that we have introduced in the book: "Opening the I's". Quite simply, you will be *informed, invited, involved,* and *inspired* to deal with the various aspects and impacts of Time Theft in your organization.

CONTENTS

Your time. My dime.

CHAPTER 1

Time Theft

Employees from all levels of an organization (from front line to executives) waste more than two hours a day at work, costing companies $750 billion a year, according to survey conducted by Salary.com and America online. Although it is not a pleasant topic to discuss, the fact is that Time Theft is costing organizations a lot of money. Workers at all levels will misuse company time at some point in their careers.

It is hard to believe that someone whom you hired to fill a trusted position in your company would actually steal from you. Nevertheless, it happens every day. In addition it is estimated that up to 75 percent of all employees' Time Theft is overlooked.

Time is money. Lost minutes result in lost dollars for businesses. In this economically challenged and competitive marketplace, every dollar counts, and every minute counts.

Survey conducted by AOL and Salary.com involved more than 10,000 respondents who indicated that there are many ways that they spend time at work doing non-work-related activities. Here are some figures from the survey:

Top Five Time-Wasting Activities

1. Surfing Internet (personal use) 44.7%

2. Socializing with co-workers 23.4%

3. Conducting personal business 6.8%

4. Spacing out 3.9%

5. Running errands off-premises 3.1%

Top Five Excuses for Time Wasting

1. Don't have enough work to do 33.2%

2. Underpaid for amount of work I do 23.4%

3. Co-workers distract me 14.7%

4. Not enough evening or weekend time 12.0%

5. Other 16.7%

Top Five Time-Wasting Industries

1. Insurance 2.5 hrs/day

2. Public Sector (Non-Education) 2.4 hrs/day

3. Research & Development 2.3 hrs/day

4. Education 2.2 hrs/day

5. Software & Internet 2.2 hrs/day

Although, *theft* is a harsh word, it is recognized by management as a significant problem. If employees take products or cash from an organization, it is considered theft. No one would argue with that. So why is it that when we talk about Time Theft—especially in this day and age when "time is money,"—we get this uncomfortable feeling? When time is money and money affects an organization's ability to make it or break it in this competitive world, then Time Theft is no different than product or cash theft. This is a simple concept, but like anything that pushes the boundaries of what we consider normal, it is surrounded by a great deal of discomfort.

Most experts would agree that *reducing* Time Theft is a much more realistic goal than eliminating it altogether. But in order to reduce time theft, business owners, management staff, and employees must recognize that the problem exists and must take an active role in preventing and controlling it.

Why Do Employees Steal Time?

People cite numerous reasons for stealing, but ultimately people steal time because they are given the opportunity to do so. When companies do not take an active role in implementing checks and balances to curb the occurrence of Time Theft, they create a fertile environment for it. When such an environment exists and all levels of employees are busy stealing time, a snowball effect is created, and Time Theft becomes part of the organizational culture.

Many employers write off losses due to Time Theft as a cost of doing business. "A certain amount of slacking off is already built into the salary structure," says Bill Coleman, senior vice president at Salary.com. But what employers might not realize is that workplace Time Theft can cost them their businesses if it isn't controlled. In August 1999 CNN Financial News reported that one out of every three companies that goes bankrupt each year does so as a result of employee theft, costing businesses between $60 billion and $120 billion a year. Although this article was referring to theft of equipment, products, supplies, etc.—imagine the cost to businesses when you add to this the losses due to time theft.

Time Theft is not confined to any one type of person or industry. The majority of executives we have talked to know that this is an issue in their company but have no idea about how prevalent and costly Time Theft really is. More importantly, they don't know how to deal with this problem.

What does this all mean to you, the business owner and an employee? Simply that you are losing hundreds and thousands of dollars every year. This stolen time translates into loss in productivity, revenue, and your competitive edge.

Setting New Boundaries

Today, Time Theft has become somewhat of a fringe benefit that employees enjoy at work. If you want your company to survive in this economically turbulent world, you need to build a culture of time-accountability. Creating a culture that respects time is vital to the success and survival of a company and it's employees.

You cannot change what you do not acknowledge.
Life Lesson #4 by Dr. Phil McGraw

CHAPTER 2

Internet Surfing Is Draining Your Bottom Line

This century has brought forward an immense digital leap throughout the developed and developing worlds. Access to information and technology, particularly the Internet, has grown tremendously over the last decade. It is estimated by Internet World Stats (internetworldstats.com) that 30 percent of the world's population (approximately 2,095,006,005 people) has access to the Internet.

How Much Is The Internet Really Costing My Company?

"Surveying the Digital Future" a report published in 2003 by UCLA provides some insights into the increasing amount of Internet usage in the workplace for both work-related and personal purposes. The report also provides data on e-mail usage for both work-related and personal matters.

Below are excerpts of the study around Internet and e-mail usage at work:

- "Of those who had Internet access at work in 2002, 60.5 percent visited Web sites for personal use."

- "About 57 percent of those who use the Internet at work in 2002 accessed their personal e-mail from work . . ."

Your Bottom Line Is Bleeding

If you are as committed to the success of your company as we are, you have already started to do some number crunching to figure out how much this personal use of Internet and e-mail is costing you on a yearly basis. But we'll make the analysis easier for you. Let's agree on some basic numbers before we provide you with the approximate costs your company is incurring due to personal Internet and e-mail use.

For the purposes of this quick analysis we'll assume the following:

- The employees in your organization make $40,000 per year.
- On average the employees in your company work 2,000 hours per year (i.e. 40 hours per week 50 weeks of the year).
- Based on the numbers above, on average an employee earns about $20 per hour.
- Each employee in your company has access to Internet and e-mail.
- On average, each employee spends approximately 2 hours per day on personal Internet and e-mail usage.

Based on the above numbers, one employee's time theft habits cost your company about $10,000 per year.

Here is the cost analysis

- 2 hours per day stolen
- 10 hours per week wasted (2 hours x 5 days)
- 500 hours wasted per year (10 hours per week x 50 weeks of work)
- $10,000 dollars lost per employee per year ($500 hours per year x $20 per hour)

Now imagine how the numbers add up when you have multiple employees in your company with the same time theft habits. For example, 10 employees with the same habits will cost your $100,000 per year. The cost increases to $1,000,000 per year if 100 employees in your organization are involved in similar non-work related activities every day.

Corporate Time Theft is here and is globally costing businesses billions of dollars every year. You will keep losing money unless you take strategic action to curb this theft problem.

Plugging the Internet Leak

Based on our experience, Internet and e-mail access at work are considered more of a necessity than a privilege nowadays. If your organization is anything like the organizations we have worked with, not using the Internet and e-mail is not an option. But that does not mean that access to these necessities cannot be monitored or controlled to yield a more productive workforce. If your organization is responsible to its investors, just imagine their reaction if they were to realize the losses due to Time Theft. Think of the taxpayer dollars lost due to this Time Theft in a government organization. However you look at it, your organization is taking a big financial hit due to this.

So what are some remedies to this problem? Here is a short list of initiatives you can undertake:

- **Information is power:** Share the Time Theft statistics with your employees. It will provide a constant subconscious reminder every time they reach out to log on to Facebook˚, shop for shoes, or catch up on the latest entertainment gossip.

- **Policy it:** Create standardized Internet and e-mail usage policies for all your employees to sign so that you can take action when these privileges are abused. Remember to refresh your employees' memories about these policies on a regular basis.

- **Designate time on company dime:** Set aside a controlled amount of time that your employees can use the Internet and e-mail for personal purposes.

- **Strike a team:** Get your employees and senior management involved in collaborating to design solutions to the problem of Time Theft. This will ensure that there is buy-in at every level. Imagine the new culture you can create within your organization by leading this change.

Time Theft due to personal Internet and e-mail use is not an issue that can be ignored. Acknowledging this issue is important in order to work towards controlling the magnitude of the problem.

Time For Change

In addition to the tangible and intangible costs, there is a significant degree of risk and liability associated with the increased time employees spend online.

With the amount of personal activities, surfing of pornographic sites, and other non-work-related activities taking place, it is time to face this workplace pandemic head on. The alternative to dealing with this issue is to turn a blind eye to continuous Time Theft and letting your organization experience the ever-growing risk of a slow bankruptcy due to lost productivity and revenue.

Internet abuse is a new and evolving problem that management has never seen or experienced before. Therefore, in order to deal with this problem, a good balance of existing and outside-the-box solutions is required. Throughout this book we have provided various solutions and ideas to combat Time Theft. This chapter provides additional solutions that may assist in the new campaign against Time Theft due to non-work related Internet usage.

Internet Usage Policies

In order to make clear what employees are permitted and not permitted to do when spending time online, organizations need to create policies and educate their employees about these policies. Aside from Time Theft, Internet usage makes organizations vulnerable to legal liabilities, ever-increasing costs for providing Internet access, threat of data loss through unauthorized access (hacking), and more.

A good Internet usage policy should cover the following items:

- The expectation that company assets such as computers, bandwidth, etc. are to be used for business purposes only
- A list of the types of Web sites (and in some cases specific Web sites) that are either blocked and/or are not permitted to be accessed
- Strictly defined prohibitions for downloading and transmitting material protected by copyright and other laws
- The consequences of Internet misuse
- Details regarding employer access to employee e-mail, Internet usage history, files, usage audits, etc.

Employees should be advised that they should not expect their communications or use of the employer's computer information systems to be confidential or private; and the organization should have every employee sign and agree to the Internet usage policy for the term of their employment. You may be thinking that your organization already does this. You're right, many organizations already have policies in place. The question is how many organizations actively enforce these policies?

Internet Workshops

One of the best and most effective ways to ensure Time Theft is controlled within an organization is to get the whole organization to take ownership of the problem. The only sustainable way this can be done is to educate the workforce on the negative effects of Time Theft due to Internet misuse. Furthermore, the organization's workforce should be involved in the creation, implementation, and monitoring of solutions.

Internet workshops are an effective way of educating employees on the effects of Internet misuse. These workshops can be used to ensure that there is complete buy-in from the employees by involving them in identifying solutions and setting operational strategies that all employees can take ownership of.

Internet workshops are also incredibly helpful in introducing new policies and codes of conducts, and in sharing information on how these policies will be implemented. Presenting employees with reports and data on the before and after scenarios will help with the critical task of getting them to see the benefits of the policies and of controlled Internet use.

Another good strategy to ensure compliance and adherence to new policies is to provide direct monetary benefits. For example, if an organization is losing a million dollars a year through Time Theft, and the implementation of certain strategies will save the company a million dollars per year, then offer to distribute up 50 percent of these savings to all employees on an annual basis for a certain number of years. This will ensure that the misuse of Internet and the accumulation of costs through Time Theft become linked directly to loss of potential income for each employee. Furthermore, this will ensure that self-monitoring and self-regulation of Internet use will come into effect right away. Of course the organization will need to ensure there are mechanisms in place to measure the changes. The good thing is that there are strategies and tools out there that can help a company with this.

R U WRKN?
I M L8
LOL
C U L8R

CHAPTER 3

Texting at Work

The face of Time Theft is changing quickly. Text messaging has become part of our daily communication. Life is getting busier by the day consequently we are all getting too busy to talk to each other, so we text instead. It is also becoming a common mechanism at work to communicate with our colleagues, clients, etc. But just like Internet usage, people are spending a lot of time at work texting for personal purposes. At the end of the day, texting at work for personal purposes on the work dime is just another way of stealing time. If it wasn't stealing, then we wouldn't think, "I hope no one sees me texting" while we text away at work.

Some experts estimate that up to half of office workers spend more time texting and e-mailing than actually working. This, according to some, is attributed to achieving a better work-life balance. In the United Kingdom, this flavour of cyber-socializing costs employers about £761 million each year.

Stealing from the workplace is more common than you might think. In fact, *you* have probably knowingly or unknowingly stolen from work. But there is a lot that can be done to prevent such theft.

The solution to minimize such Time Theft issues can be as simple as instituting a well-documented cell phone and text messaging policy derived with collaboration between management and staff; management should follow up on this policy by calling a staff meeting to communicate the policy to employees as something that they have played an integral part in creating. An even better approach is to sit down with each staff member individually and review the policy carefully, making sure that each member of the team fully understands the policy and the consequences of violating it.

Formalizing policies to curb such work distractions is a crucial part of ensuring that your employees understand the culture of the organization. A collaborative approach at the work place will also help in changing the culture of the organization in the long run.

If the abuse of cell phone usage on company time has been severe, consider implementing a "no cell phones" policy. Of course this approach will only work in environments where cell phones are not an integral part of the business interactions.

As with any new policy, the key is consistency. Always enforce the policy and follow through with consequences when necessary, even if it means penalizing a top performer or terminating someone. This shows the rest of the staff that you are serious, and it sends a strong message that it is unacceptable to steal company time.

In the end, your consistent application and enforcement of the policy will determine its success. Having a formal policy for cell phone use at work will give your associates more time to take care of clients and focus on the business.

Let's help others be honest employees.

I like working between breaks.

CHAPTER 4

Breaks Breaking the Bank

What is the number one spot in your workplace for socializing? Historically, in most businesses it has been the water cooler. Now the most socializing probably occurs as we stand in line for our favorite caffeine drink and chat with our co-workers. And here is the kicker: all this is done on company time. This is one example of everyday Time Theft in action at your company.

According to a Salary.com survey, in general employees waste 20 percent of every workday. Based on this number, 1.6 hours of an eight-hour workday are wasted by employees every day through activities such as taking unscheduled coffee breaks, watching the news, reading magazines, making personal phone calls, and text messaging, etc. In a five-day workweek the average employee wastes more than an entire workday. Note that we are not saying that an employee *can* waste an entire day; we are saying that an average employee, believe it or not, *does* waste an entire day of work by taking part in non-work-related activities at work during work hours.

Think about all the activities that are potentially eating away at your profits and productivity and in turn increasing your costs. There is no shortage of things people can do at work if no one is keeping track of their activities. Some of the leading time-wasting activities employees take part in at work (other than Internet use) include:

- Socializing with co-workers
- Conducting personal business
- Making personal phone calls
- Taking extended breaks to run errands

Here are some more interesting facts that researchers were able to collect. According to a survey men and women waste time equally. Good to know there is gender equality in Time Theft.

Unfortunately, there isn't age equality in Time Theft. Younger employees are inclined to waste more time than older employees. Employees between the ages of twenty and twenty-nine reported the most wasted hours at work. Are you ready for the figure? They self-reported 2.1 hours a day wasted on non-work-related activities. How many employees do you have between the ages of twenty and twenty-nine?

In comparison, the average time wasted for employees between the ages of thirty and thirty-nine was reported to be 1.9 hours per day, whereas employees between the ages of forty and forty-nine wasted an average of 1.4 hours at work each day. These are numbers that affect all organizations, including yours.

There is no doubt that a minute today is worth more than a minute was five, ten, or fifteen years ago. Time Theft in an organization, if not controlled, will affect the profitability and sustainability of an organization. Times are changing and how we deal with Time Theft has to change with time.

There is a lot that can be done to change employees' work habits, but nothing can be done without the vision, commitment, and investment of time and resources from people like you. The alternative is watching employees swap entertainment gossip over extended coffee breaks and watch Time Theft be added to the list of employment benefits offered to all your employees and co-workers. We all know what that will lead to—especially in this economy.

As you may have noticed, we try to use statistics to convey our message to you. Adding some hard numbers to these statistics will show you how much these unscheduled breaks on average cost your company. Many people do not realize how much these stolen minutes affect the bottom line. Let's re-create the habits of an employee (we'll call him Joe) who wastes a lot less than the average of 2 hours per day. As you review the numbers below, imagine how easy it is for employees to engage in Time Theft on a daily basis. Let's look at Joe and his daily habits where he:

- Extends his break by five minutes
- Extends his lunch by five minutes
- Goes out for 4 smoke breaks of 5 minutes each (20 minutes)

Tally of stolen minutes:

- Daily wasted hours per day: 30 minutes (0.5 hours)

- Weekly wasted hours (based on a five day work week): 2.5 hours
- Yearly wasted hours (based on fifty weeks of work): 125 hours

The bottom line:

- As in earlier examples in this book, let's assume that on average your employees earn around $20 per hour.
- 125 hours of wasted time per year are costing you $2,500 every year.
- If your company has more than one employee who is taking part in this self-directed employment benefit, the financial impact is even bigger. The figures below demonstrate how this dollar amount multiplies as the number of employees increases:
  - o Ten employees wasting 125 hours per year costs you $25,000.
  - o Fifty employees wasting 125 hours per year costs you $125,000.
  - o One hundred employees wasting 125 hours per year costs you $250,000.
  - o Five hundred employees wasting 125 hours per year costs you $1.25 million.

Shocked? Join the club. Keep in mind that the numbers noted above are based on less time than what employees generally waste. Now imagine that *your* employees are wasting on average 2 hours per day every day. Time Theft is a multibillion-dollar industry. So, are you ready to change things for the better?

Hey, boss! Do you know the cost of your own breaks? This is a private assessment of your nonscheduled breaks.

Time Theft: Self Assessment	
Daily wasted hours:	
Monthly wasted hours:	
Yearly wasted hours (A):	
Average hourly rate (B):	
Total $ wasted: (A) x (B)	
Total $ wasted by you:	

Now let's do a quick assessment of Time Theft and its costs due to breaks by members of your team/department/staff.

Time Theft: Team/Department/Staff Assessment	
Number of team members/staff (A):	
Daily wasted hours per person:	
Monthly wasted hours per person:	
Yearly wasted hours per person (B):	
Yearly wasted hours by team: (C) = (A) x (B)	
Yearly wasted hours by your team (C):	
Average hourly wage per person (D):	
Total $ wasted by team/department/staff: (C) x (D)	
Total $ wasted by your team/department/staff:	

The change starts with you. Time Theft stops with you! Are you ready?

If you had to identify, in one word, the reason why the human race has not achieved, and never will achieve, its full potential, that word would be "meetings."
Dave Barry

CHAPTER 5

Meetings: Less Is More

Throughout the book you will notice that we talk about the importance of culture change within an organization to curb Time Theft. This chapter brings to light how a company's culture directly fuels Time Theft in an organization.

As you go up the executive ladder, you spend more of your time in meetings. More than twenty million meetings take place in the corporate world daily, and most meetings are from one to two hours long. Some people complain that they cannot get their work done because they have to spend too much time in meetings. This is a common problem at all levels of an organization. We are sure you experience the same sentiments quite regularly.

How often have you sat for over an hour in a meeting that was going nowhere and felt your anxiety level rise as you thought, "I am sitting here when I could be doing something else. This is a waste of time."? And you are absolutely correct. Meetings that are off base are definitely a waste of time. Even worse, they are a tremendous waste of money. Think of it as legalized Time Theft in an organization.

Even though we have all heard "Meetings are useless" so many times, have you ever thought about why people actually feel that way? There has been a lot of research conducted to find out what it is about meetings that people despise so much. We want to share these common complaints so that you can incorporate strategies in your meetings to eliminate some, most, or all of the issues people have with meetings. The end results will yield a greater appreciation for meetings within your company, and better yet, will save you a ton of money!

According to research there are a lot of reasons that people hate meetings. Below we have listed a few of these issues:

- Poor preparation for the meeting by the organizer and attendees
- No agenda or too many items on the agenda
- Time allotted to agenda items unrealistic
- No prioritization of agenda items
- Ineffective facilitation
- Meeting objectives unclear
- No prior background about issues/topics being discussed
- Too many participants
- Key decision makers not present, etc.

Often the biggest expense is the salary of the people who are attending the meetings. Do you know how much meetings cost you? Here is a hypothetical scenario that shows some basic numbers to help you grasp the magnitude of meeting costs:

Costs of average meetings:

Average hourly salary of attendees	$20/hour
Number of attendees per meeting	7
Average length of the meetings	1.5 hour
Average number of meetings per week	5
Cost of meetings per week	$1,050
Cost per year (50 work weeks)	$52,500

Now imagine that your organization has ten departments with similar meetings costs. These meetings will cost you on average about $525,000 per year. If you have twenty departments that meet in the same pattern, these meetings will cost you over $1 Million per year. The costs are even larger when you take into account that on average, depending on the position of the person in an organization, they are likely to have an average of 2 meetings per day.

Meetings are a necessary evil. But there are proven methods that can help you save money by controlling this type of Time Theft. Here are four ways you can control the cost of meetings:

1. **Justify:** Ask yourself, "Do we really need to meet?" If the answer is no, then cancel the meeting. If the answer is yes, then think about the next three points

2. **Reduce:** Cut down meeting lengths. For example, reduce the duration of a meeting from 1.5 hours to 1

hour. This will require you to create a focused agenda for each meeting and ensure that active facilitation is taking place.

3. **Eliminate:** Cancel at least one meeting per week. This will require you to review the validity of your meetings.

4. **Evaluate:** Ensure that only people who need to be at a meeting are at that meeting. If a larger group of people need to know the decisions from the meeting then invest time in creating minutes and circulate them to the larger group.

After implementing these four strategies you will conduct shorter, more focused meetings and save a lot of company money. Here is an example of the potential impact:

Costs of meetings after implementing cost-saving strategies:

Average hourly salary of attendees	$20/hour
Number of attendees per meeting	5
Average length of meetings	1 hour
Average number of meetings per week	3
Cost of meetings per week	$300
Cost per year (50 work weeks)	$15,000

As noted earlier in this chapter, department meetings can cost up to $52,500 per year per department. By reducing the number of attendees, number of meetings, and the length of the meetings, now one department meeting potentially costs $15,000 per year yielding a saving of $37,500 per year. If ten departments in your organization implement the same strategies, you could save up to $375,000. If twenty departments in your organization implement the same strategies, you can save $750,000. Just imagine—the time this would put back into your employees' hands to take part in more productive activities that actually help in increasing your bottom line.

Meetings have been around for as long as companies have been (if not longer). Changing your employees' perceptions of meetings will not be an easy task., but it *is* possible to make a positive change. By committing to controlling meeting costs, you will see short-term and long-term time and cost savings.

Action indeed is the sole medium of expression for ethics.

James Adams

CHAPTER 6

Workplace Ethical Standards

Ethics is derived from the Greek word *ethos*, which means "way of living." Ethics is a branch of philosophy that is concerned with human conduct, more specifically, the behavior of individuals in society, the workplace, and at home.

Workplace ethics refers to the body of moral principles and values held by an individual employee—anyone from the frontline staff to the CEO. Ethics is a funny little thing. It matters most when no one is looking. So when no one is looking at work, are you doing your work?

Attention to ethical standards in the workplace is making a strong comeback due to the increased pressure for accountability and transparency at all organizational levels. Shareholders want to know exactly what is going on. Taxpayers want to know that their tax dollars are being used properly. Customers want to know that they are dealing with organizations that are transparent. Employees want to know that they are working for organizations that operate within ethical frameworks.

One of the first things that President Barack Obama did was to create a list of ethical guidelines for his administration. Right away that sent a message to everyone that indeed change was coming. President Obama wanted to create these ethical guidelines to ensure that he and his administration and staff would be accountable and transparent to the people whom they serve.

Ethics don't stop at governments. Our actions and decisions at work, home, and anywhere else—regardless of whether anyone is watching over us—are the true indicators of our ethics.

The bottom line is that at work we are being paid to do work, increase revenue, provide services to our customers, or meet other business goals. We are being compensated to do something in exchange for money. So if we are spending two hours every day surfing the net instead of doing the work you are being compensated to perform, shouldn't that set off our internal ethics alarms?

The reason we wanted to discuss ethics in connection with Time Theft is that, as we work on bringing to light the impact and damage caused by Time Theft in our organizations and businesses, we will come across many attitudes and rationales. You will hear things like: "My manager is on eBay all day buying things for his home," or "My co-workers are always logged into Facebook," or "I get tired of looking at work all day. Everyone needs a break." All of these excuses point to a growing notion of entitlement. But the fact that some people feel they are entitled to do something doesn't make it right. So as we work toward limiting the occurrence of Time Theft, we will have to work very hard to ensure that everyone affected by these changes understands the underlying ethical boundaries that are crossed when stealing time.

Have you formulated a code of business conduct for your organization? A code of business conduct applies to all workers from top to bottom. It enables a culture that facilitates workplace ethics, a "walk the talk" attitude, transparency, and accountability, while providing well-defined boundaries for all members of an organization.

Let's consider an extreme example involving sexual harrassment. Even such an obviously unethical action as sexually harassing someone at work requires a written sexual harassment policy in thousands and thousands of organizations! So don't you think Time Theft warrants a written Appropriate Use of Company Time policy in your organization? If you don't come out and acknowledge the problem and put forward collaborative solutions to facilitate a culture change in your organization, then you may as well close up shop. You are losing money. You are losing time. The buck stops with each one of us. With downsizing and job cuts, every organization is being asked to do more work with fewer people. If we are expecting fewer people to do more work, then shouldn't we ensure that the time being spent at work is being utilized to do work?

A policy not only articulates the dos and don'ts of an organization, but more importantly, it delivers a mechanism to show an important part of the organization's ethics and values. But quite frankly, a document is useless if the essence of the policy is not lived out by the people in your organization or enforced by your organization. Creating an Appropriate Use of Company

Time policy (i.e. Time Theft policy) for your organization will be wasted effort if the masses in your organization at every level are not on board. Of course any policy being created with regards to the appropriate use of company time would also have to recognize the facts within the company, such as:

- work environment
- type of work
- level of tracking and reporting in place
- work hours and handling of overtime
- compensation method, etc.

A policy document could outline topics such as:

• Refraining from handling personal business matters during work time

• Refraining from engaging in extended socializing at the workplace on company time

• Refraining from using company time to engage in personal Internet use and telecommunication activities during work time

• Being responsible and doing no harm to the company

• Protecting the interests of the company and its development ("Saving the company saves jobs.")

• Reporting violations of work time abuse

• Handling personal work hours reporting with integrity and honesty

• Effective time management

- Making responsible choices, setting a good example, and being a role model

As employees of a company it is our responsibility to establish a practice of positive time ethics in the workplace. These ethical standards should be developed collaboratively and put in writing. A company may also choose to provide ethics training and guidance to its employees on an ongoing basis.

A leader has the vision and the conviction that a dream can be achieved. He inspires the power and energy to get it done.
Ralph Nader

CHAPTER 7

Keeping Four I's on Time

So here we are, sitting at the intersection of "I know something needs to be done about Time Theft" and "I am not sure what to do, when to do it, and how to do it." Fear not my friend! This intersection is a heavily visited, widely known, and an often ignored one, but with the right navigator, you will be on your way to reducing and even eliminating Time Theft in your organization.

Reading through the previous chapters, you have a better idea of the flavours and impact of Time Theft. Now you will start to notice occurrences of Time Theft every day in your work life and in other aspects of your life. Congratulations! We have opened your eyes to Time Theft. This is a great thing because now you are tuned into the problem and more importantly to the opportunity to make some changes. If you're anything like us, you are already thinking about how to solve this Time Theft problem quickly. This is where we are going to put on our "We have done this before hat" and talk to you about a few things you need to ensure are in place before you start to think about any drastic changes.

We love analogies, so what better way to explain what we are trying to say? Here goes: Think of the habits of the people in your organization as a fast-flowing river. We'll call it Theft River.

Imagine that you're standing on the banks of the river watching the water flow faster than you have ever remembered it to flow. You have an urge to jump into the river and create an obstruction that will slow or even stop the river flow. But you know as well as we do that this river has been around for a long time and has seen many obstructions in its way. Those obstructions are long gone and forgotten, and the Theft River still flows. With the serious problem of Time Theft, you surely don't want to be just one of those things that tried to curb the flow of the river and was swept away by its force. What you need is a watertight strategy that is sustainable, manageable, and adoptable.

We know that this is not a task that can be completed overnight, but we also know that it is not an impossible task either. Honestly speaking, you are a pioneer in your organization, and you must take the leadership role in creating a "stimulus package" for your organization by curbing the effects of Time Theft.

We all know that there is no leadership when there is no ship for the leader to lead. So step one is getting people on board using our tried, tested, and true strategies, that we call the Four I's for Change. Let's look at the I's in more details.

Inform

The first step in getting anyone in your organization onboard with an idea is informing them about it, specifically in this case, regarding the concept of Time Theft and the effects it has on an organization's bottom line, culture, and productivity.

Look at yourself as an example. Is your mind buzzing with ideas about curbing Time Theft? Information empowers. Once you share information, you not only empower others but you empower a culture of change.

These four things will help you inform others:

1. Socializing the concept of Time Theft
2. Communicating the positive impact of eliminating Time Theft
3. Sharing ideas of how everyone can help to eliminate Time Theft
4. Starting with sustainable and manageable changes through proven strategies or by engaging experts to help you with this

Invite

In order to ensure that everyone is onboard, you must inform as many people as possible through information sessions, newsletters, and a variety of formal, informal, verbal, and written methods. Now is the time to invite people to join this movement toward becoming a time-ethical organization. This will provide the momentum you need to ensure that you are able to influence change on a larger scale.

The more people you inform and invite to help, the better and faster you will see changes taking effect.

Involve

This is the key step. Skipping this step is where organizations lose the pulse of their organizational culture. There are two ways to approaching a solution to a problem in an organization:

1. Senior leadership can dictate the solutions
2. The organization can inform, invite, and involve people from all levels of the organization to create solutions

Needless to say, we believe that involvement of people within the organization yields many positive results. The most important effects of this involvement are:

- creating immense positive energy to curb Time Theft;
- securing complete buy-in from all members of the organization;
- establishing full ownership by everyone involved; and
- making a smooth cultural transition to a more efficient, effective, and time-conscious culture.

And these are just the organizational behavior benefits. Just imagine the financial benefits that will come out of this! Truly speaking, controlling Time Theft in an organization is like finding an untapped gold mine. Of course you will need to provide some incentives for people to be involved in this change so they see some personal benefits as well as organizational benefits by changing their behaviour.

Inspire

As much as we as authors are adamant about curbing Time Theft everywhere, the only reason we can stay charged up about this idea is because both of us were at some point inspired. And now the results we see every day in our lives as we reduce and eliminate Time Theft in our work and other aspects of our lives keeps us inspired and motivated.

As an agent for change, you will need to work on ensuring that during the process of informing, inviting, and involving, you are also inspiring people around you to change. This inspiration can be provided using many methods. By far the most effective one that we have seen is taking on the responsibility of setting a good example for everyone around you.

Once you start to talk about Time Theft all eyes will undoubtedly be on you. People will be watching and waiting to be inspired (or disappointed) by your actions. Hey, no one ever said that being a leader is easy! But once you get over that initial effort, you will notice that your actions will set into motion a grand momentum of change that will be perpetual and will become an integral part of the organization's culture.

We see this leadership behavior all the time. It is based on the Time Theft mantra: "I better get back to work." Over tea one day we were discussing how this "I better get back to work" culture is addictive and permeates an organization completely; and we began talking about one employee who loved to talk to anyone and everyone in sight. One day this person started one of these long conversations with one of us and just kept talking. A couple of minutes into the conversation, this person heard something that she had never heard before. She heard "I better get back to work. We should talk about this during our next break because it sounds really interesting." All this employee could do was quietly absorb what was said and nod her head in agreement.

What an impact this little encounter had on her! The very next day we noticed that another one of this employee's co-workers was engaging in a long, drawn-out conversation. The normally talkative employee looked at her co-worker and calmly said, "I better get back to work; otherwise I will be here 'til late. How about we go for coffee on our break and you can tell me all about it then?"

Don't get us wrong—there will be people who will never understand this concept of change and would love to hold on to their old ways of doing things. The key is to inspire enough people around them to change so that the hard-to-change people have no choice but to gracefully integrate themselves into the new culture.

While writing this book, we heard about one of our mutual acquaintances who was notorious for wasting time not only by not doing his own work but also by walking into others' offices and just chatting. Guess what? After many little encounters that should have made him aware of his time-wasting habits, he still didn't get it. So now he is unemployed. The organization decided to streamline its team, and the first person whose name came up for the chopping block was his. We think people don't notice; but trust us, people notice our actions.

So the question is this: are you ready to keep four I's on Time Theft in your professional life?

We must become the change we want to see.
Mahatma Gandhi

CHAPTER 8

I Better Get Back To Work

What do you do when someone insists on talking to you while you are trying to do your work? Do you become complacent by being polite and letting them continue to steal your time? Or do you tell them that you need to continue with your work? A large majority (if not all) of the people in this situation will wear a smile and let their time tick by. We know what you *want* to tell your co-worker, and we also know that you end up not telling them what you feel. How do we know? We have been in your shoes.

Six little words will help you get back on track with your work: "I better get back to work." Just imagine being in a situation in which all you can think of is getting back to your work while a co-worker is busy wasting your time. Now think about how you might try get out of such a situation. You might look at your watch and say something like, "Wow, it's two o'clock already? Where does the day go? I better get back to work; otherwise we'll both be here 'til night trying to catch up on our work. Can we talk later?" What do you think the other person's response will be? We can tell you. The other person will come out and agree with you 100 percent.

Not comfortable? Well, let's practice. It may sound silly, but it will help. Go on and practice saying "I better get back to work" three times as you look in the mirror. See? It's not that hard.

You may still have a little bit of uneasiness, but think about what you have just done. You have not only reclaimed your time, but you have also started a chain reaction within your organization starting with your co-worker. You are becoming an agent for good change.

Change is not easy. It will not be easy for you, and it will not be easy for others. But it is important to realize that you are making this change to make your organization better, more profitable, and more successful in these trying times.

The foundation stones for a balanced success are honesty, character, integrity, faith, love and loyalty.
Zig Ziglar

CHAPTER 9

Loyal Employees

Loyal employees are those who have made an emotional commitment to remaining with your business for the long term. These employees are creative; they look for ways to serve the organization and to satisfy customer needs. Loyal employees are dedicated; they go out of their way to create extra value for customers and for the organizations they work for.

It has been said that the creation of loyal employees is both a science and an art. The top five drivers of employee loyalty are

1. the care and concern that the employer shows for workers;
2. the fairness of pay;
3. management's appreciation for employees' ideas and input;
4. an employee-focused atmosphere; and
5. professional and personal development opportunities.

The real loyal workers are the ones who will go that extra mile to delight customers and who are highly motivated in their work. These employees are "here to stay" with your organization.

Strength in Loyalty

At the end of the day even your most loyal employee is still influenced by the culture of the organization. Loyal employees probably have the best of intentions for their organization; but working within an organization where Time Theft is the norm may have moulded the practice of this loyalty over the years. In other words, over the years they may have inadvertently evolved into becoming Time Thieves.

Breaking the cycle of Time Theft in your organization will require you to reach deep inside the organizational culture and light a spark of change for the better. To achieve this, one of the greatest allies you will ever have on your side are your organization's loyal employees. These employees have grown with the company, they have seen good years and bad. They understand what it takes for a company to survive in such tough economical times. It is important that you spend time to get the loyal employees on board with your mission against Time Theft. Through their influence with others in the organization and by setting a good example for other employees, these loyal employees will continue to provide the extra push required to change your organization's culture.

These loyal employees have invested a lot of time, effort, and passion into your company over the years. They share a special bond with the company and through this special bond they are fully invested into the company's survival and success. Make sure that you involve these loyal employees as they will provide not only their commitment but also insight into the organizational culture that you may not already have.

No matter how noble the cause, you are still stealing time.

CHAPTER 10

The Balance

Work-life balance is more than just a buzzword or something that high-power motivational speakers preach. It is a fine balance of what we want to do, what we need to do, and what we have to do. In order to achieve work-life balance, it is inevitable that you will need to establish priorities among things like career, family, hobbies, leisure activities, personal time, etc. As we move faster than ever before and get busier than ever before, active participation in the creation of work-life balance has become a necessity.

In this day and age, we all know that work and non-work time blend together so much that it is hard to tell whether certain times are for work or for family. More than ever before, workers play many different roles in their lives. They are employees, parents, spouses, friends, caregivers to elderly relatives, volunteers in their communities, etc. They must also make room in their lives for taking care of their own physical and mental well-being. Not surprisingly, achieving balance among all these competing priorities can be difficult. In fact, more than half of working people report an overload associated with their many roles.

Now throw into this mix the accessibility of new technologies meant to make our lives easier. These technologies—e-mail,

BlackBerries, and iPhones, for example—are more like electronic leashes that encourage the expectation that we will be available 24/7 to everyone around us. With these pressures and the expectation that we will fulfill so many roles, it is no surprise that work-life balance has become the elusive Holy Grail.

Achieving work-life balance means establishing equilibrium among all the priorities in one's life. This state of balance is different for every person; however, as difficult as work-life balance is to define, most of us know when we are out of balance.

We are not alone in feeling that we are spending more time at work than with family, this is a common feeling according to a study that examines the time Canadian workers spend with family members during a typical workday. The study, published in *Canadian Social Trends*, found that on average workers spent forty-five minutes less a day with their families during workdays in 2005 than they had two decades earlier.

Work-life conflict occurs when the time demands imposed by work and personal life become incompatible with one another. People start feeling that there is not enough time in a day to do all the things they need to or want to do either at work or in their personal lives.

The Essence of Time and the Bottom Line

You must be wondering why the authors are bringing forward the topic about work-live balance in a book that is geared towards helping organizations save money and potentially increase their revenue. In our experience, there is a direct correlation between the amount of Time Theft an organization experiences and state of the work-life balance of the employees of that organization. Through this chapter we hope to help you learn more about your own work-life balance so that it helps you understand the state of your organization's employees' work-life balance. And in doing so, we hope you will see how the imbalance between work and life can affect the occurrence of Time Theft in your organization.

There is no easy way to achieve the balance; we have to make an effort, starting with taking an inventory of all the things we do in a day. Think of it the same way you think about financial planning. Not too many people like doing it, but everyone knows that it is important to do. The same is true when it comes to our time.

Let's start by looking at how George spends an average twenty-four hour day and how he can prioritize the things he does in order to have time for everything he wants to do.

George's Day

Activities	Typical Day (hours)
Sleep	8
Work/School/Home	8
Grooming	1
Eating	2
Commute	1
TV	2
Phone	30 minutes
Internet and e-mail	1
Food (buying/cooking)	30 minutes
Cleaning, washing, etc.	
Appointments	
Reading	
Family time	
Hobbies	
Friends	
Fun/Activities	
Love/Romance/Sex	
Other:	
Other:	
Other:	
Other:	
Total	24 hours

You can see that a lot of other things that George wants to do or needs to do in a day just don't get done. So where you do think the time to get these things done will come from? When we have so many demands on us and our time, we are automatically inclined to "borrow" (i.e. steal time) from wherever we can. Statistically, that time stealing most often occurs at work from work hours. In some cases, more than two hours are stolen from a typical workday.

Are you ready to evaluate your typical day at work? Take a few minutes to fill out the blank timesheet in this chapter. This will help you take an inventory of your entire day and your hours at work. This is the first step in achieving work-life balance and evaluating where you stand on the Time Theft scale. Based on what you see, you can prioritize your day to fit in whatever you want and need to.

Your Average Day Timesheet

Activities	Your Typical Day (hours)
Sleep	
Work/School/Home	
Grooming	
Eating	
Commute	
TV	
Phone	
Internet and e-mail	
Food (buying/cooking)	
Cleaning, washing, etc.	
Appointments	
Reading	
Family time	
Volunteer work	
Hobbies	
Friends	
Fun/Activities	
Love/Romance/Sex	
Other:	
Other:	
Other:	
Total	

Your Average Workday Timesheet

Activities	Productive Time	Non-Productive Time
Late Arrival		
Quick hallway chats		
Checking and replying to work e-mail		
Checking and replying to work voicemails		
Checking and replying to personal e-mails		
Checking and replying to personal voicemails		
Extended coffee break		
Other work-related items		
Extended lunch		
Extended chats		
Internet surfing (including Facebook®, Twitter, etc.)		
Personal text messaging		
Other personal business (homework, social planning, etc.)		
Other:		
Other:		
Other:		
Other:		
Total		

Enter the totals from the table "Your Average Workday Timesheet" above into the table below. This will give you an idea of how your average workday is structured.

Your normal paid hours per day	
Your total productive hours per day	
Your total non-productive hours per day (time stolen from your company)	

So, based on the numbers above, if the time stolen from the company is a positive number, you have to get creative about how you are going to make up for that stolen time. Are you going to steal time from someplace else? That someplace else is your family time and/or your personal time. This is where the vicious cycle of imbalance begins to affect your personal life as well as your company's bottom line.

Many organizations have now started to learn more about their employee's state of work-life balance. Companies have started to invest more actively in their employees' well-being to ensure that their people are happy, healthy, and lead a balanced life. Has your organization started to do the same? We hope that this chapter has helped you not only learn more about your work-life balance but has brought you closer to understanding why employees in your organization may be stealing time. Remember, it's not always good to think about what employees can do to make an organization better; it is also about how an organization can help make it's employees better.

The purpose of this book was simple: we wanted to quantify the prevalence of Time Theft, teach you how to identify it, and give you the strategies to contain it. Keep in mind, at the end of the day the strategies you employ to fight Time Theft in your organization will directly impact other people. So be gentle, conscious, and empathetic in your approach.

ABOUT THE AUTHORS

Grace Chandy, MBA, HRA, CMC

Grace Chandy has over thirty years of experience in health care management, and leadership. As a visionary and a change agent, Grace shares her leadership knowledge through consulting services, seminars, and strategic planning for a wide array of corporations and stakeholders. She is the author of Topnotch Leader and Undiet Lifestyle. She also mentors and coaches to help others recognize their true potential. Grace currently resides in the beautiful city of Vancouver, Canada.

Zen Tharani, BSc., PGCert

Zen Tharani is a Managing Partner at a leading health informatics and information technology consulting firm. Specializing in the field of health informatics, Zen has and continues to provide his expertise to clients through consulting engagements around the world.

An avid believer in and an advocate of building strength in community through volunteering and mentorship, Zen spends much of his time involved in community initiatives. Zen enjoys contributing his time and knowledge by mentoring others and by sharing the knowledge and skills he has gained through his own mentors. Zen currently spends his time between Vancouver, Victoria, and Regina in Canada.

CORPORATE
TIME THEFT

You Can't Afford to Ignore It

To help organizations recognize, reduce, and control Corporate Time Theft, authors Grace Chandy and Zen Tharani are available to conduct various types of sessions for senior management, business owners, and staff.

To invite the authors to speak at your organization or to conduct seminars and workshops at an event, please contact us via e-mail at: help@ibettergetbacktowork.com

You can order additional copies of *Corporate Time Theft* by visiting:

www.ibettergetbacktowork.com

Or by visiting our publisher's bookstore website:

http://www.trafford.com

ACKNOWLEDGEMENTS

Special thanks to all those who have knowingly or unknowingly contributed their thoughts, experiences, and support to this book. We apologize if we haven't been able to acknowledge all the contributors formally.

NOTES

NOTES

_____

_____

_____

_____

_____

_____

_____

_____

_____

_____

_____

_____

_____

_____

_____

_____

_____

_____

_____

_____

_____

_____

_____

NOTES

NOTES

_____

_____

_____

_____

_____

_____

_____

_____

_____

_____

_____

_____

_____

_____

_____

_____

_____

_____

_____

_____

_____

_____